101 Reasons to Visit Israel

(& perhaps make aliyah)

ESTIE AND DOVID SOLOMON

ARTZY BOOKS
JERUSALEM • NEW YORK

101 Reasons to Visit Israel

Published by ARTZY Books

Cover and Book Design: **Benjie Herskowitz**

Editorial and Production Manager: **Daniella Barak**

Soft Cover ISBN: 978-1-934440-02-5

Email: sales@ARTZYBooks.com

Printed in Israel

IN MEMORIAM

In loving memory of Mrs. Finne Mandelcorn, a"h

Faige bas Mordechai Nisson

פייגא בת מרדכי ניסן

Table of Contents

Acknowledgments

First and foremost I would like to thank my dear husband, Steve, who had the vision and backbone to come on Aliyah to Israel, for his constant support in this endeavor.

I thank my dear mother, Mrs. Hanna Tennenhaus, and my amazing brother, Rabbi Yisroel Tennenhaus, who selflessly gave me their blessing to go on Aliyah even though we'd see each other less often.

I thank Mrs. Freda Solomon, my dear mother-in-law, for coming on Aliyah a year ahead of us. I thank HaShem for my wonderful children, children-in-law, grandchildren, nieces and nephews who fill me with joy. Their *middot* and lifestyle make me proud. I hope one day they too will come to Eretz Yisrael.

I thank my youngest son, Avrohom Dovid, for spending his Tuesday afternoons taking many of the beautiful pictures in this book. I want to thank you, Ilene Kahan, for contributing three special pictures to the book. I thank the computer maven, Neshama Ruth Kane, for putting this book in order. Last but not least I thank Mr. Yaacov Peterseil at Devora Publishing Company for encouraging me to publish this book.

Introduction

The land of Israel really does not need introduction. It is the inheritance of all the Jewish people in all generations for all times. I made Aliyah in August 2004 with my husband, Steve, and son, Avroham Dovid. Then we encountered firsthand our true heritage.

In Eretz Yisrael, people are less concerned about the size of their house or car than they are about how many hours a week they can devote to learning Torah, spend time with their families, and participate in charitable activities within their communities.

There is a passion for life here and a great capacity for joy. Despite the hard work, large families, and political uncertainty, when Shabbat and the *chagim* arrive, the excitement in the air is palpable.

The Torah comes alive with visits to the Holy sights where our ancestors were years ago. Faith is strengthened when you see a Talmudic village 2000 years old that is complete with a synagogue and *mikvah*. Every time I see these historical sights, I think, "Moses is true and his Torah is true."

Chapter 1

The Life for Children

Children are celebrated here in Israel. Having a family is both a mitzvah and a Jewish value. Most women work outside of the home, and there is a large support network of child-care providers.

The school day is shorter in Israel than in the Diaspora, and children fill the afternoon with their favorite activities, such as computer lessons, gardening, sports, art, science labs and much more.

Also, each month children are taken by their schools on *tiulim* (field trips) to learn Jewish history first hand.

You and your newborn can enjoy a vacation

AT THE MOTHER AND BABY CONVALESCENT HOME IN TELZ STONE

Working moms:
Your baby will be well cared for in a large selection of *ganim* day care centers in Israel

VERONICA AND MIRIAM'S GAN IN ZAYIT, EFRAT

Your children will receive an excellent and affordable Jewish education

בנק מסד
166 2821
ירושלים
ידידי ביה"ס מקור חיים-649
חשבונית מס 282110426
עוסק מורשה
סולומון
אברהם
הרב ברלין 2 ב
מס פנימי
תשלום עבור שכר לימוד
סכום לפני מע"מ. 380.00
מ.ע.מ. 0.00
סה"כ 380.00
הסכום נגבה מחשבונך מספר
תשלום מס 5 מתוך
נכון ל 02/01/2005
חתימה

 OUR TUITION BILL FROM MEKOR CHAIM SCHOOL, JERUSALEM

Your children will be at the controls of a spaceship

THE MARS EXHIBIT AT THE BLOOMFIELD SCIENCE MUSEUM

You'll take your children on meaningful historical field trips

THE ENTRANCE TO THE CAVE OF THE PATRIACHS IN HEVRON

Your sons
and daughters
can play
roller hockey
in an
after school
chug

LIBERTY BELL PARK IN JERUSALEM

Your children can enjoy a popular activity known as *kerameka* (pottery design and painting)

It is pleasing to see beautiful playgrounds with swings and slides in most neighborhoods

A COMMUNITY PLAYGROUND IN MODIIN

WATER PARK IN TIBERIAS

1.10 — ROCK CLIMBING

Your older
and bolder
offspring
can go
rock climbing

SIMULATION ROCK-CLIMBING WALL IN NORTHERN ISRAEL

1.11 — BBQ SEASON

You can prepare family BBQs nine months out of the year

1.12 – MINI ISRAEL

You and your family will be able to walk through Israel in two hours at Mini Israel

A LARGE PARK WITH MINIATURE MODEL SITES AND BUILDINGS FROM ALL OVER ISRAEL

You can celebrate your son's Bar Mitzvah at the Kotel

 ELI AND EITAN REINER'S BAR MITZVAH CELEBRATION

Chapter 2

Shabbat and Holidays

In the weeks leading up to the major Jewish holidays, there is a hustle and bustle in all the shopping areas. Holiday decorations and treats are seen everywhere.

Traffic slows down with the arrival of Shabbat. The supermarkets close by 2 P.M. and the streets become quiet and empty.

Many people can be seen dressed up in their best clothing, maybe pulling along a suitcase or two, as they travel to visit family or friends to celebrate Shabbat together. They may be going to another city or to participate in a weekend Bar/Bar Mitzvah party.

Many Israeli families open their doors to host students and visitors for Shabbat. The hospitality is a story within itself... Everyone's apartment stretches to fit the number of guests at the table.

You can even donate food on Shabbat for needy families

 DROP BOXES LOCATED THROUGHOUT ISRAEL

2.2 — THE POST OFFICES ARE CLOSED ON SATURDAY

You will notice that most businesses, stores and government offices are closed on Saturday and open on Sunday

THE RECHAVIA POST OFFICE ON KAREN KAYEMET L'YISRAEL

2.3 — QUIET IN THE STREETS

You will experience a wonderful serenity during Shabbat in many neighborhoods

MEAH SHEARIM AT FIFTEEN MINUTES BEFORE CANDLE-LIGHTING

2.4 — KAPPAROT

You will be able to perform the *kapparot* ritual right on the street the day before Yom Kippur

A BOOTH SET UP ON STRAUSS STREET, JERUSALEM

2.5 — LULAV AND ETROG

You will be able to purchase a beautiful lulav and etrog from a street vendor

MALCHAI YISRAEL STREET, JERUSALEM

You may choose between a 100 interesting places to visit on *chol hamoed* Sukkot

NAOT KEDUMIM PARK HAS MODELS OF ALL THE SUKKOT MENTIONED IN THE MISHNAH

You will see that even Jerusalem's City Hall has a large *sukkah*

CITY HALL, JAFFA STREET, JERUSALEM

2.8 — HAKOFOT

You can dance with a live musical band at *Hakofot Shneot*, the night after Simchat Torah

THE BANDSTAND AT LIBERTY BELL PARK, JERUSALEM

You will experience the joy of lighting your menorah outdoors in special glass cases

RAV CHEN STREET, RECHAVIA

You will see lots of strange costumes on the street

MALCHEI YISRAEL STREET, GEULA, ON PURIM AND SHUSHAN PURIM

You will find large pots of boiling hot water on many street corners in which to kosher silverware before Passover

FROM THE GARDEN IN FRONT OF THE SHTEIBLACH SHUL, KATAMON

2.12 — ONLY ONE SEDER

You will experience only one Passover seder. All the holidays are one day except for Rosh Hashana

THE SOLOMON FAMILY'S SEDER TABLE IN EFRAT

2.13 — MIMOUNA

You may participate in a Sephardi *mimouna*

2.14 — LAG B'OMER

You will be able to participate in an all night bonfire

ON LAG B'OMER, EVERYWHERE IN ISRAEL

Chapter 3

Nature

The country of Israel is breathtakingly beautiful. The large oceans, the high mountains, the low valleys, the bright flowers, and the perpetual blue sky make Israel a popular vacation destination. You can begin your day in the north with a sleigh ride on top of Mount Hermon; if you travel eight hours south to Eilat, you can swim in the sea that evening.

You can climb by a foot path or ride up in a cable car to the top of Masada

You can see a myriad of colors and varieties of flowers throughout Israel

A GARDEN NEAR KING GEORGE AND AGRON STREETS

3.3 — THE BEACHES

You can have a lot of fun or relax at the many beaches in Israel

AN ASHKELON BEACH FRONT

3.4 — THE BLUE SKY

You will
smile up
at the
blue, blue sky

You will be able to go white water rafting near an Israeli waterfall

 THE TEL DAN NATURE RESERVE, NORTHERN ISRAEL

You can get into shape on any of Israel's many walking trails

You might want to vacation in Tiberias, where the Sanhedrin once sat

You will see spectacular views all over the country

VIEW SEEN FROM LIFTA OVERLOOKING RAMOT, JERUSALEM

3.9 — EILAT

You can go for a quick getaway weekend in Eilat

 ROYAL GARDENS HOTEL, EILAT

3.10 — JUDEAN HILLS

You will see the picturesque Judean Hills

THE VIEW FROM THE SOLOMON FAMILY'S WINDOW IN EFRAT, GUSH ETZION

You will witness the breath-taking sunsets

Chapter 4

Spiritual Learning and Development

There is a tingly spiritual feeling that comes over most people as they walk through the streets of Jerusalem. The lively sights, sounds and scenery that surround a person make him or her keenly aware of what a privilege it is to be in Israel.

To the east, west, north and south of the land there are ancient sights and treasures, historic proof of the existence of our forefathers. A visit to any of the holy sights will rejuvenate your soul.

4.1 — PRAYING AT THE KOTEL

You can *daven* at the Kotel as often as your heart desires

KOTEL PLAZA, JERUSALEM

You can choose from a large selection of synagogues and *mikvaot*

THE FOUR SEPHARDI SYNAGOGUES, OLD CITY, JERUSALEM

4.3 — RABBI SHIMON BAR YOCHAI'S GRAVE

You can pray at the holy sights (i.e., the enclosed grave of Shimon Bar Yochai)

You will have a better understanding of our heritage

THE RUINS OF THE ANCIENT VILLAGE OF KATZRIN WHERE THE MISHNAH WAS COMPILED

9.5 — HONOR THE ELDERLY

You will find the biblical quote "for the elderly you stand up"

THIS IS POSTED IN ALL THE EGGED CITY BUSES

You may attend interesting learning groups all over Israel

THE ORTHODOX UNION ON KEREN HAYESOD HAS ALL DAY TORAH CLASSES AND ACTIVITIES

You can walk in the footsteps of our ancestors

THE PATRIACHS ROUTE LOCATED IN NEVE DANIEL IN THE GUSH ETZION TORAH STUDY

You may participate with the thousands of students studying Torah daily

MIR YESHIVA, JERUSALEM

4.9 — GRAVES OF THE MOTHERS

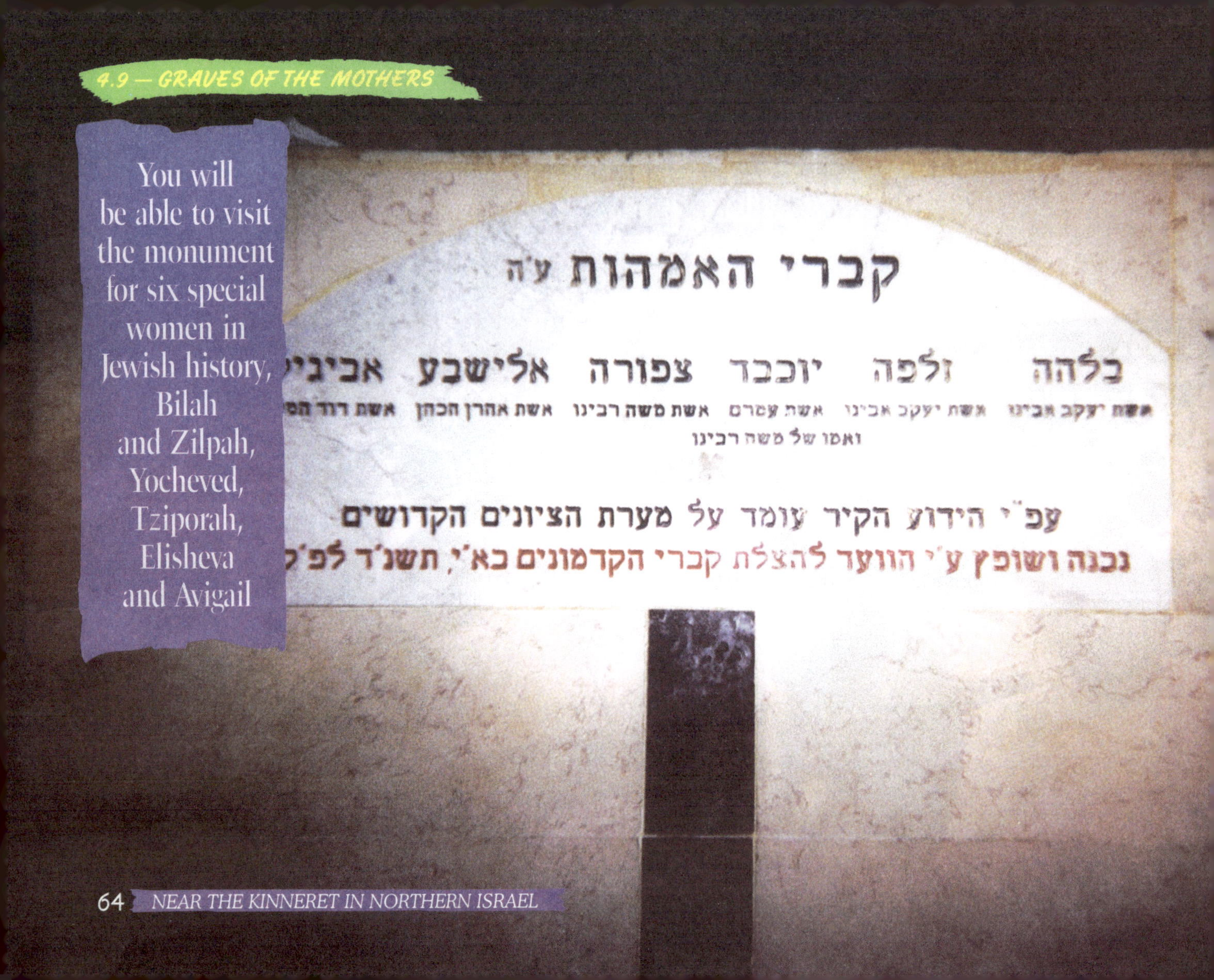

You will be able to visit the monument for six special women in Jewish history, Bilah and Zilpah, Yocheved, Tziporah, Elisheva and Avigail

Chapter 5

A Great Selection of Kosher Food

We know that the tourists enjoy delicious food at hotels and restaurants when they visit Israel. The huge Israeli Breakfast, which includes pancakes, tuna, cheese and vegetables, keeps most tourists filled until dinnertime. This chapter is filled with kosher goodies that the average Israeli can buy. It is deliciously enjoyable to be able to stop while doing errands and have a kosher meal or snack.

Three basic food items are low in cost due to government subsidies: rye bread, dairy products and chicken.

You will taste *rugelech* and cheese Danish that are exquisite

 NA'AMON BAKERY ON THE CORNER KING GEORGE AND JAFFA, JERUSALEM

You will be able to choose from a large selection of delicious fresh fruits and vegetables

THE SHUK, MACHENE YEHUDA, JERUSALEM

5.3 — WINE

You can find a large selection of kosher wine even at the local grocery store

 SHOP ON AZZA STREET, JERUSALEM

You can enjoy *hafooch* coffee (latte)

You will find amazing salad bars in most restaurants

You can sit
and have
a kosher meal

5.7 — LACHMANIOT

You will love the fresh, crispy breads and *lachmaniot*

A BAKERY OUTSIDE OF THE MACHENE YEHUDA ON JAFFA STREET

You can buy by the "kilo"

5.10 — ICE CREAM

You can choose between low-calorie soft ice cream, or regular ice cream treats

KETZEFET ON BEN YEHUDA, JERUSALEM

You can enjoy mid-Eastern kosher falafel and shawarma

MOSHIKO RESTAURANT ON BEN YEHUDA, JERUSALEM

Chapter 6

Lifestlyes

The morning starts early in Israel. Most children arrive at day care or school by 8:00 A.M. and parents are heading to work.

Some businesses close in the afternoon and reopen in the evening when the weather is cooler. The main meal is served at lunch, and supper is usually a light dinner consisting of pita, salads and dairy products. There are interesting classes, lectures and entertainment to attend most evenings.

Celebrations such as weddings and Bar/Bat Mitzvahs are often held outdoors in the summer months when there is rarely rainfall.

You can still buy beautiful apartments in many towns in Israel

 THE MANDELCORN FAMILY IN BEITAR

You will love the Egged bus service. It's super fast

THE PARKING AREA OUTSIDE THE OLD CITY WALLS IN JERUSALEM

You may choose from excellent universal medical insurance

 MEUCHEDET IS ONE OF FOUR NATIONAL HEALTH COMPANIES

You will get brand-name medication for less

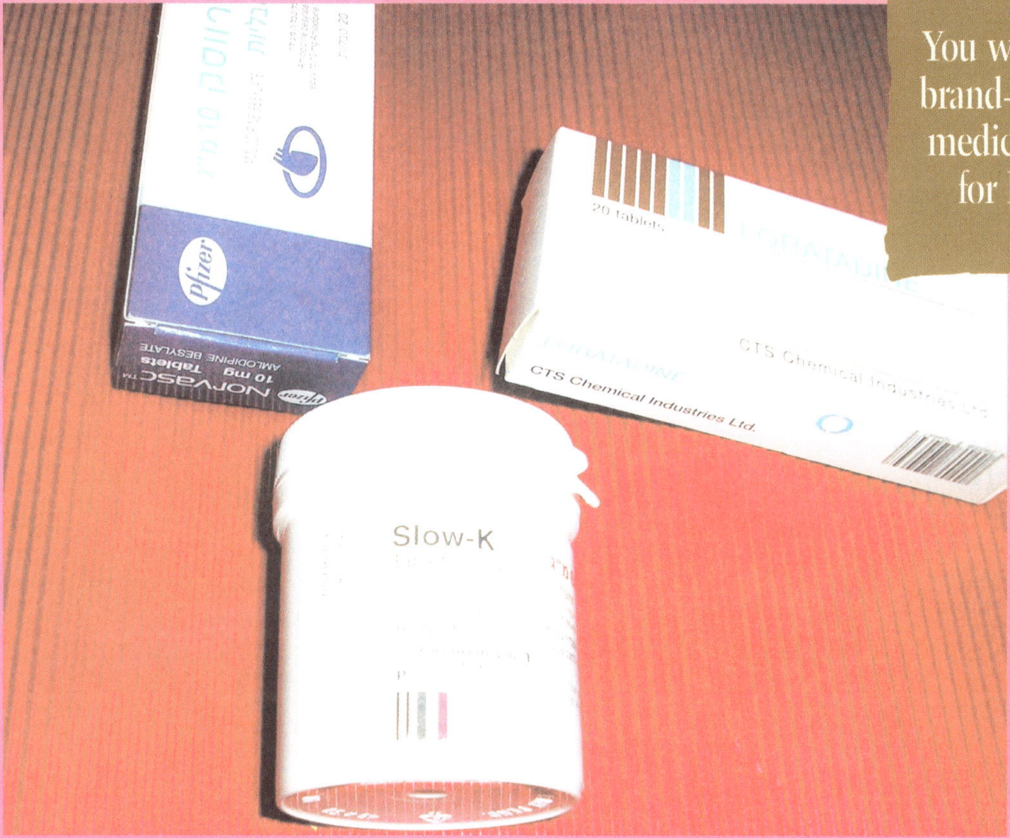

6.5 — HEBREW CHECKING

You can write a check in Hebrew

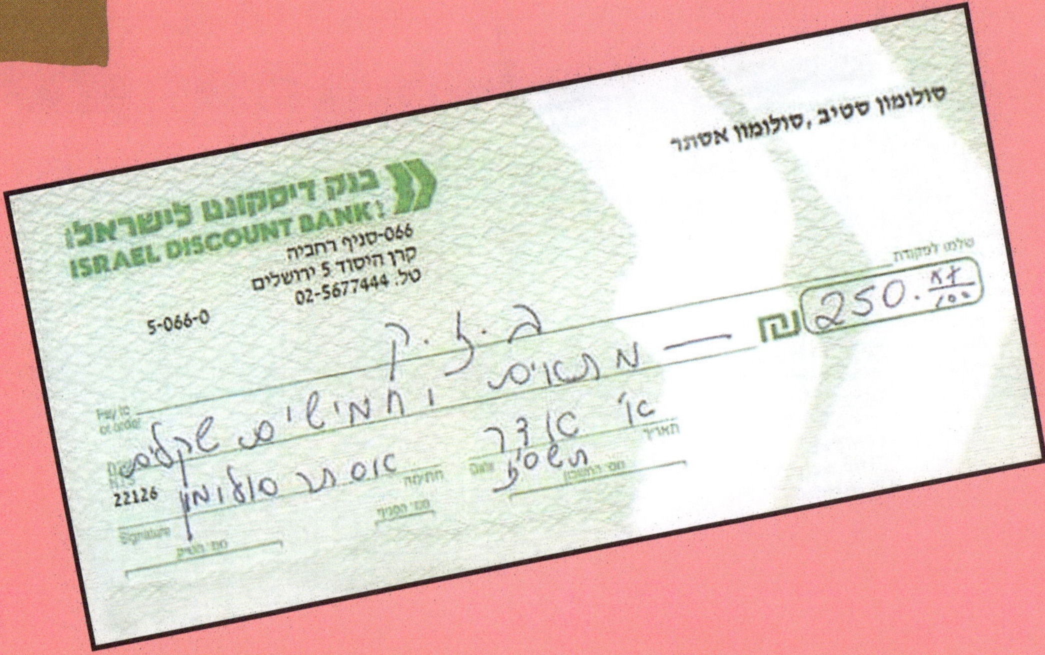

Your dollar will go a long way (most of the time)

6.7 — HEBREW IS THE NATIONAL LANGUAGE

You will learn Hebrew as a language used in everyday life

NO SMOKING SIGN

You will enjoy the cultural scene

A PLAY ABOUT THE GUSH KATIF EVACUATION AT THE BEHAR THEATER IN JERUSALEM

You will celebrate Sukkot as a national holiday; schools and universities close down for the week

THE HEBREW UNIVERSITY CAMPUS, HAR HATZOFIM

You can get married in front of the Patriachs

PREPARING A CHUPA IN FRONT OF THE CAVE OF THE PATRIACHS IN HEVRON

You can join a cause that will make a difference to the Land and its People

50,000 PROTESTORS AT A RALLY ON CHOL HAMOED PESACH

You can be a one-man non-profit organization

SERVING COFFEE AND CAKE TO OUR SOLDIERS AT A PINA CHAMA (WARM CORNER)

6.13 — BOOKSTORES ON ALMOST EVERY BLOCK

You can be part of the people of the book

 STEIMATZKY'S BOOK STORE

You will enjoy visiting many interesting museums

THE ISRAEL MUSEUM, JERUSALEM

Take the Jerusalem tour bus and see the major sights in one day

 THE 99 BUS ROUTE BEGINS NEAR THE CENTRAL BUS STATION AND STOPS AT 25 LOCATIONS AROUND THE CITY

You can visit a kibbutz and experience a country lifestyle

KIBBUTZ KFAR ETZION IN GUSH ETZION

6.17 — NATIONAL PROTECTION AND PRIDE

You will hear the youth of Israel pledging allegiance to their country

CEREMONY FOR NEW RECRUITS AT THE KOTEL

You may meet your *bashert* (match) here

MIA TEPPER OF NEW YORK MARRIES SHMUEL LEW OF RANAANA

Chapter 7

Considering Aliya?

Here are four words of encouragement – You can do it!!!

Every Jew of the Diaspora has the knowledge and skills to integrate into life in Israel. Using computers, the Internet, faxes and voice-over-Internet lines, many olim maintain their North American jobs.

Today, it is easy to stay in touch with loved ones all over the world.

You will receive free assistance from several organizations that help with the aliyah process

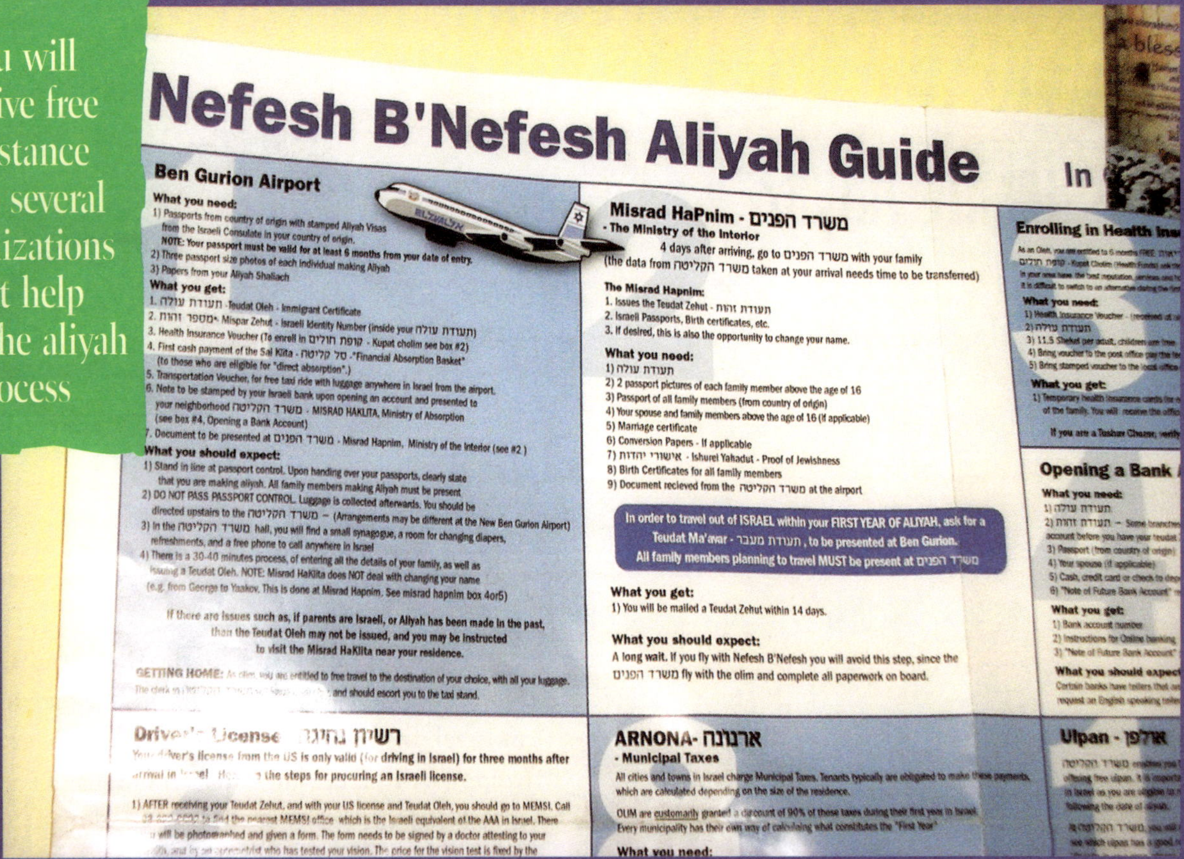

 NEFESH B'NEFESH, THE JEWISH AGENCY, AACI AND OTHERS ASSIST WITH INFORMATION AND PAPERWORK

You will learn to read and speak Hebrew at a local ulpan with qualified instructors

MITCHELL'S ULPAN, TALBIAH, JERUSALEM

You can become an official Israeli citizen

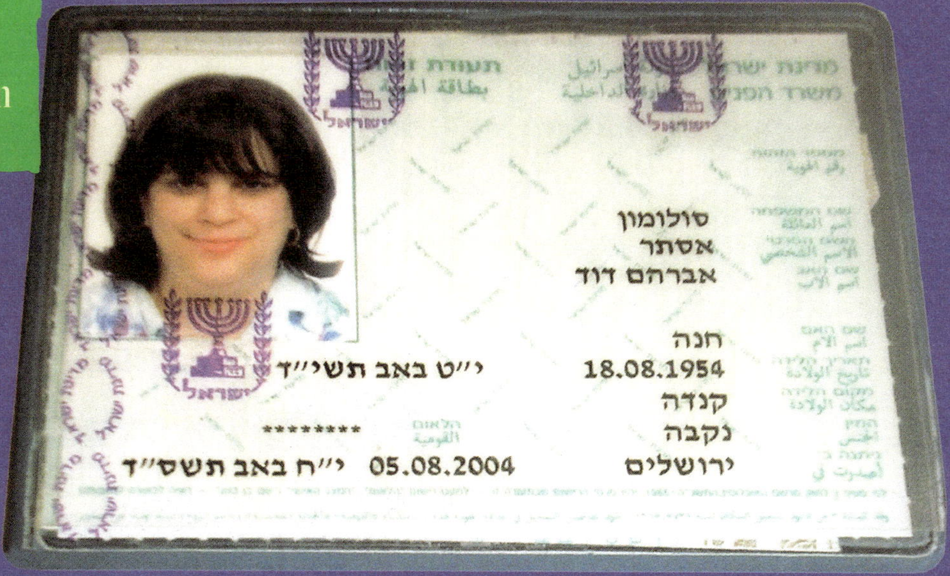

7.4 — JOIN TOGETHER IN PRAYER

You can find a minyan wherever you go

PRAYING MINCHAH IN THE STREETS OF HEVRON

7.5 — SHABBAT DISHWASHER

You can buy a dishwasher with a Shabbat cycle

7.6 — ALL FOR ONE

You will be part of the ingathering of the Jewish people

INSIDE THE GATE NEAR THE KOTEL PLAZA

7.7 — KNESSET

You can vote for one of more than 20 Jewish parties

THE KNESSET BUILDING, JERUSALEM

7.8 — ISRAEL UNDERSTANDS SECURITY

You will feel more secure at the malls, restaurants and other public places

SECURITY WITH A SMILE ALMOST EVERYWHERE

7.9 — SINGING SOLDIERS

You can visit an army base and hear the soldiers sing; on the battlefield and off, our soldiers have inner strength

You may discover family you never knew you had

THE BROWN FAMILY ALL TOGETHER

You will be coming home when you arrive on aliyah

 BEN GURION AIRPORT, LOD, ISRAEL

Chapter 8

Places to Go and Things To See in Gush Etzion

We were excited to find the ancient City of Sussia that dates back to the 4th – 9th century. Located one-half-hour by car from Hevron in a remote area, it is the largest ancient community in the area. Its remnants include a shul, a *mikvah,* water cistern systems, the ruins of houses, as well as a large underground shelter complete with shelves for food. It is not known when or why the city was abandoned. It the excavation started in 1984 and is continuing to the present day. There are many interesting and beautiful sights to see in this area.

You can learn firsthand how Kosher wine is produced

8.2 — ANCIENT SYNAGOGUE

You can visit the remnants of the Sussia synagogue that was used from the 4th to the 9th century

SUSSIA IS A 45-MINUTE DRIVE FROM CHEVRON

8.3 — MOSAIC TILED FLOORS

You will see how Jews in ancient times decorated with tiles

SYNAGOGUE FLOOR IN SUSSIA, HISTORICAL MUSEUM

You will learn about the struggles of settling in the Gush Etzion area

You will see beautifully decorated, modern-day synagogues in the resettled Gush Etzion

BEIT HAKNESSET NETA BENYAMIN (RABBI RISKIN SHUL), EFRAT

8.6 — ANCIENT MIKVAH

You can find *mikvaot* from 2000 years ago to *tovail* in

NEAR ALON SHVUT ON THE ROAD OF THE PATRIARCHS

You may have to wait in traffic for a few minutes while a shepherd and his sheep cross the street

ON THE ROAD NEAR BETHLEHEM

Chapter 9

Favorite Sights

Israel has so much to offer. No visit to Israel is complete without participating in some of the activities depicted in this chapter.

For example, twice a year – on *chol hamoed* Succot and Pesach – thousands of people gather for the *Birkat Kohanim* (the Priestly Blessing) at the Kotel Plaza. For those two mornings a year, all the thousands of people from all Jewish perspectives pray in unison with one loud and clear voice.

An hour south of Jerusalem, you can float in the Dead Sea where minerals in the water help heal many skin and rheumatic conditions.

9.1 — BIRCHAT KOHANIM

You can be part of the thousands who pray together in unison at *birchat kohanim*

KOTEL WALL, JERUSALEM ON THE 3RD DAY OF SUKKOT AND PASSOVER

9.2 — THE WINDMILL

You will discover Montifiores' legacy in Yemin Moshe, the first neighborhood outside of the Old City

YEMIN MOSHE WINDMILL, JERUSALEM

You will find great bargains and treats in the *shuk*

9.4 — BAIT YAACOV

You can see the first religious girls school in Israel

9.5 — OLD TRAIN STATION

You will be able to see many art exhibitions at the old train station

You can purchase from a large selection of original Judaica that reinforces Jewish tradition

You can visit Ashkelon historical park to learn about the ancient history of that area

9.8 — YAM HAMELECH

You can visit the lowest point on earth

YAM HAMELECH (THE DEAD SEA), ISRAEL

Conclusion

I used to think, "A coffee, a bagel and a newspaper – it doesn't get better than that!"

Everyday is exciting and special here in Israel. The beautiful scenery and the potential for learning in classes, as well as sightseeing or just walking through the streets, accompany the realization that Jews from everywhere are coming home.

Yes, a coffee, a bagel and a newspaper are good, but my new life post-Aliyah gives me a spiritual high. Whoever reads this book, and is inspired to come and visit, you are welcome to be my Shabbat guest.

Sponsors

Mrs. Leah Raso – A special friend who found her way to Eretz Yisroel in 1989. She divides her time between Israel and Montreal.

Mrs. Frede Solomon – She made Aliyah in 2003 at age 75 and is living happily in Jerusalem at Ramat Tamir Seniors Residence.

Mr. and Mrs. Mordy Feiner – A young couple studying Torah in Jerusalem in 2006 and 2007

About the Authors

Esther Solomon born in New Brunswick, Canada, grew up in Montreal, Quebec. Prior to making Aliyah, Ester worked as a community health nurse in Canada and in the USA. In Israel, Esther works as a Lactation Consultant, using her International License IBCLC. She is an avid reader, loves cooking – especially for Shabbat, and writes in her spare time. She created this book after moving to Israel in 2004.

Since school closes early in Israel on Tuesday afternoons, her 12-year-old son, Dovid, who is a 7th grader at Bet Hamedrash Ohr Torah Stone in Efrat, took his camera and went with Ester to take pictures of beautiful sights around the country.

Her husband is Rabbi Steve Solomon, a well-known Jewish community social work director, and she is the mother of six beautiful children, four lovely children-in-law and many, many grand-children – may they all be well. She now lives in Efrat with her husband and Dovid. She goes back to visit the rest of the family two to three times a year.

My Reasons for Visiting Israel

My Reasons for Living in Israel